INTRODUCTION

The team at Child Care Biz Help is honored to share a compilation of ideas to help child care centers get noticed as they target both candidates to recruit and families to enroll. We hope our ideas help relieve some of the pressures you're feeling and all you are juggling.

We have walked in your shoes and as we continue to work with child care centers, it has become apparent, you need more support than ever. Thankfully, we are very passionate about what we do and we want to help you succeed and overcome the daily obstacles of both enrollment and recruitment.

Enjoy our tips and tricks as you read through 1,001 very different strategies. Try just one or attempt all 1,001!

Go have fun, love what you do, life is too short.

ISBN: 9781079109689

First Edition 2019

Co-write by Caroline Jens, Justina Paterson, Crystal Towler, Cover and design by: Dana Breunig

TABLE OF CONTENTS

COMMUNITY OUTREACH

1. Partner with a local ice cream shop, hand out free ice cream coupons at the store and give materials about your center to anyone you can.

2. Participate in NAC Night (National Night Out-Neighbors Against Crime).

3. Partner with your local school district. Get to know their needs and determine ways you can support them - even if it is just to bring them "survival" treats.

4. Participate and attend local festivals/kids' events.

5. Partner with a local sub shop and hand out free subs or discount coupons.

6. Partner with a local gym/fitness center and invite them to host a class for current parents (parents bring a buddy).

7. Host an infant massage classes for the public.

8. Partner with a local library to support events focused on literacy with children.

9. Host a winter party/public open house - snowman building contest.

10. Donate Easter eggs to the area egg hunt with info/candy/toys in them.

11. Volunteer to have a "Giving Tree" at your center and partner with local outreach services to give to families in need.

12. Host a brat fry at a local grocery store, donate proceeds to area library.

13. Make care packages for local first responders & invite them to your center and provide them treats.

QUICK TIP

When out in the community, wear shirts with your logo and take lots of pictures and videos to post on social media. Tag the business and people you visit.

14. Host a school supplies drive. Partner with an outreach program to collect school supplies for those in need.

15. Organize a team of teachers/parents and do a March of Dimes walk.

16. Make care packages for military oversees over holidays - ask if current families have any family members you can directly send to.

17. Sponsor a team or collect money for a team at your center and walk on behalf of Autism.

18. Get involved in local 4th of July festivities- have families dress up and walk in parade and hand out "goodie" bags.

19. Have the Fire Department come to center to do a safety training. Consider a weekend training so families can attend the event.

20. Join your local Chamber of Commerce.

21. Join your local Kiwanis/Jaycees/Lions Club and have a member of leadership involved.

22. Trick or Treating with four & older classrooms at local nursing homes.

23. If your community hosts a tree lighting during the holidays, sponsor part of the event (Santa, cookies, fun giveaways).

24. Visit your local nursing homes to sing songs anytime of the year.

25. Ask a pediatrician to come talk about child development; open it up to the public.

26. Partner with a local business that aligns with yours and do a giveaway. This could be with a grocery store, hair stylist, gym, other kid or family friendly business near yours.

27. Spotlight a different local business each month, give them a shout out for what they do great and put some flyers up at your center.

COMMUNITY OUTREACH

28. Host a Saturday event in your parking lot with carnival activities; invite food trucks.

29. Host a community luncheon once a month.

30. Ask to read stories at the library to mom's groups.

31. Host a community walk to support causes like breast cancer or leukemia. Get sponsors and donate the money.

32. Participate in a Relay for Life event in your neighborhood as a team.

33. Start a book club for moms.

34. Host a Saturday afternoon tea party for moms.

35. Partner with a different organization each year for Camp children to "volunteer" some time - use as a field trip.

36. Sponsor a craft area at a Breakfast with Santa event; Have your teachers work it and provide coloring pages with your logo.

37. Ask to be featured at your bank, they have spotlight tables, take advantage.

38. Enter a float in the holiday parade, give away fun candy/toys/swag (Frisbees, beach balls, sunglasses).

39. Give out Popsicles/snacks at local splash pad with other "swag" to recruit new families and teachers.

40. Sponsor a Movie in the Park. Come with games, tattoos, face painting and other fun things for the children to do before the movie starts.

41. Host a mini golf tournament on your playground/grass/parking lot. Hold after hours and offer prizes to those who get hole in ones or the most strokes; open to public.

COMMUNITY OUTREACH

42. Pick a charity each month and donate to them; Have the kids donate the money in a charity jar for the month to help train on giving.

43. Partner with local bank to have a banker come talk to your families about starting a saving plan/college fund for their child and tips on how to get started.

44. Have an audiologist come to your center after hours and do hearing screenings for children.

45. Partner with local OB/GYN and mid-wives to cross-market each other.

46. Host a virtual webinar later at night (think after typical bed time) about hot-button topics and invite parents/community to attend.

47. Donate branded prizes/gift basket to local fundraisers.

48. Cook breakfast at a local woman's shelter.

49. Hand out water bottles wrapped with center information for at local run/walk event.

QUICK TIP

Don't be shy to ask a local business to cross-market with you. You never know how you can help each other.

50. Sponsor a senior and work with a senior home to give back to the community; share your stories about your relationships between the kids and the seniors.

51. Host a trunk or treat event in your parking lot during the month of October; invite the community; have teachers and families decorate their trunks and give away prizes.

52. Host a chili tasting contest and allow the outside community to attend and judge.

53. Work with your local gym and host a cycle-a-thon so you can raise money for a special cause.

COMMUNITY OUTREACH

54. Host an everything is chocolate event! Create a special invite to attend it!

55. Organize a "fun run" where everyone dresses goofy. It's a great even to get your center name out there and a unique team building opportunity.

56. Participate in Red Nose Day and raise money for its cause.

57. Participate in the trike-a-thon and allow children to bring their own bikes from home.

58. Become a wish granter and help grant wishes for the Make A Wish Foundation.

59. Restaurants like Chick Fil A have family and education nights where you can bring some staff and participate. Invite your families and make it a fun night. What else is going on in your community?

60. Partner with Habitat for Humanity and work with them to build a home on the weekend.

61. Ask your staff to volunteer as a team at a homeless shelter around the holidays.

62. Participate in Toys for Tots; consider doing it during the summer so children have fun things to do over the summer time.

63. Host a center rummage where you raise money to donate or to purchase new things.

64. Have the children make holiday cards or valentine cards and deliver to the elderly.

65. Sign up when children's events are happening at County Zoo to have a booth or be able to hand out brochures or goody bags to families.

66. Get backpack swag made. Donate to local churches for back to school.

67. Mentor young moms to give them support.

68. Plant a tree and blog on the impact on the environment and our children.

69. Honor rescue personnel. Bring baked goods to the local police station.

70. Donate to clean yards or shovel for seniors.

71. Host a cooking podcast for working moms.

72. Partner with Big Brothers' Big Sisters.

73. Host a community rummage on a Saturday in the parking lot. Charge $20 per spot to have a booth and then you orchestrate all the advertising.

74. Work your State's child care association to be part of the advocacy actions they do to help ensure you keep your pulse on the child care industry.

75. If you organize a scholarship program for the high school, consider having parents as part of the selection committee. Donate even just $500-$2,000 a year to a nearby school.

76. Host a pancake fundraiser at local restaurant and donate proceeds.

77. Have a fitness trainer host a wellness event on a Saturday.

78. Sponsor a hole at your Chamber golf outing. Have something fun for the golfers to do when they are at your designated hole like a diaper changing contest.

79. Sponsor your local high school football team or just sponsor the water for the games.

80. How can you help make a shopper's experience at the mall more enjoyable during the holidays? Have your teachers wrap gifts for free; give out treats.

81. Offer to read stories at your local bookstore once a month.

COMMUNITY OUTREACH

82. Work with foster family groups to offer flexible services to these families.
83. Partner with a local eye doctor for vision testing at your center for families and the community.
84. Host seminars for newly pregnant moms and families. Incorporate how the center can help them during and after the pregnancy.
85. Host a Lamaze class at your center after hours.
86. Host a dad's group since many dads are now homemakers.
87. Work with church youth groups and consider donating money for events to help those kids that can't afford to do things.
88. Provide free gifts to new moms and dads at the hospital to make the birthing process a little easier.
89. Work with the military community to support families.
90. Sponsor soldiers oversees as a center or even Wounded Warriors Group.
91. Support a local orphanage and even consider mentoring some of the children.
92. Work with local Girl Scout and Boy Scout groups.
93. Think about donating your service or your product to charity auctions. Not only is this great to help others, you can network, meet probable customers, and increase your local profile.
94. If there is a mom's group in the neighborhood that meets on a regular basis - offer to buy the group lunch or breakfast on behalf of your center.
95. Partner with a local barber/hair salon and offer haircuts to families at the end of the day (in center) or discounts for weekend visits at their business.
96. Ask a Speech & Language Pathologist to come talk about development - open it up to the public.

97. Volunteer at Halloween events in community - donate pumpkins for pumpkin patch (if they have one).

98. Sponsor a team in the local 5k (at any time of the year) and run/walk together, be sure to get t-shirts!

99. Have an ice cream social in your parking lot - have the ice cream donated and tag the ice cream shop on social media for their support.

100. Host a summer party/public open house.

101. Create yard signs for current families to put in their law "proud member of..." - Make them colorful yet keep the verbiage simple and large.

102. Host an event for Grandparents Day.

103. Host a "Muffins with Mom" event.

104. Host a "Donuts with Dad" event.

105. Host a "Date Night" event for current families - parents can drop off kids for specific time to have a "date night" - provide pizza & movie. Show pictures on social media.

106. Host a CPR class at center for expecting parents after hours.

107. Host a general CPR class for parents who want to stay current.

108. Host 'shopping' days during the holidays - "Drop & Shop"

109. Host a family movie night during the summer on your playground; encourage your families to bring other families.

QUICK TIP

For events at your center, consider offering them both in the morning and evening to accommodate a variety of schedules families may have.

FAMILY EVENTS

110. Organize a scavenger Leprechaun hunt at your center to look for the leprechaun during March.

111. Organize an Easter egg hunt and other activities for current families and open to public.

112. Host an after hours Thanksgiving dinner. Have each age group be responsible for a food group. Consider having this event as an open house.

113. Host a Book Fair / Pre-K Open House event for current families and prospective families.

114. Host an 'Ask the Experts" event at your center where parents can come and ask the teachers about handling situations with children.

115. Find a nook or other small space in your entrance and create a coffee bar with a hashtag and encourage parents to share pictures of them on social drinking the coffee.

116. Host a "wine and paint" event for families to attend after hours.

117. Host a diaper drive at location to donate to local shelters or outreach programs.

118. Invite the local fire department and offer fire extinguisher training (put out actual fires).

119. Survey your families each year on events they would like to you to host.

120. Create a present to give to families to say, "thank you" (i.e., an oven mitten w/ wooden spoon and cookie mix, DIY ornament kit, kids' t-shirt with logo).

121. Coordinate a project you can do with your families to improve your center (i.e., playground, classroom painting, garden); share progress and create hype about it.

122. Teach the community on important child milestones that should occur from birth to age five.

123. Do any of your parent's blog? Find out if they'll promote your location on their site.

124. Contact a local photographer to partner with that will come in and take pictures of the children, offer special family sessions on the weekend. Nice pictures, discounted rate.

125. Bring in a dermatologist to talk about the safety of being in the sun before summer hits (give little goody bags of sunscreen and information) - open to the public.

126. Participate in the book it Give-Me- 20-Program; Set goals for your center, celebrate your success. bookitprogram.com.

127. Host an Art Auction and have children paint pictures and auction them off. Donate proceeds to local charity or use as a fundraiser for improvements to facility.

128. Host a "Family Feud" night at your center where families pair up with each other - take video for social media/website.

129. Host a "Christmas around the world" event during the holidays. Have each classroom pick a country and do a craft or cook food based on that country.

130. Make sure your staff makes Father's Day, Mother's Day, Grandparent's Day, Christmas, Valentines, Birthday cards/gifts for their parents/grandparents/guardian.

131. Instead of a date night out, offer for families to come, bring their children and spend time together for a "parent night in event."Try a theme: game night, movie night, book night.

132. Schedule a family outing to a local farm, local country fair, or baseball event. Don't forget shirts. Try to get corporate/group rates on tickets.

133. Never stop enrolling families!

134. Don't be afraid to ask for donations from local establishments, give away the donations as gifts to families. Tag them on social!

135. Don't give up! Sometimes, not every marketing strategy works the first or second time. Keep at it...it will pay off.

136. Hire a professional photographer to come in and get quality pictures of your staff and children in action. Use on marketing materials and website. Be sure to get releases for the children.

137. Hire a professional videographer to record a video about what makes your center special.

138. Design colorful and informative banner flags and put outside property advertising enrollment - go bold and colorful!

139. Establish your core values- Define them, Display Them, Live by them.

140. Analyze your logo, is it time for a face lift?

141. Do you use Procare? Did you know you can change the photo on the check in screen? Put upcoming events or specials on there for all to see!

142. Respond to online inquiries in a timely manner (within an hour) during business hours, don't wait days!

143. Create a calendar each year of the marketing things you are doing so you can plan ahead of time. This will make your efforts exponentially easier.

144. Set enrollment metrics for your team to hit! When you have a goal, it's very motivating. Consider adding a bonus structure for these goals.

145. Determine your USP (unique selling proposition) if you haven't already; this allows your staff to more easily sell how you are different than the competition.

146. Get backpacks/shirts for summer camp. They will wear them to every field trip and be walking advertisements. Put your logos all over them.

147. Make small holiday appropriate changes to your logo (holidays-add lights, St. Patrick's-turn green, valentines-add heart, etc.).

148. Host a day where the students teach. Call it Opposite Day!

149. Get paper straws made with your brand. See if the local water park will use them.

150. Sponsor a banner at the water park. Make sure to call people to action! Our center makes a huge splash in the lives of Kids!

151. Ever advertise on a bus or on the subway? Try it!

152. Advertise with Uber or a taxi service! Great place to have an ad!

153. Advertise at the baggage claim at the airport is amazing! People sit there forever!

154. Get branded fanny packs! They are back in style!

155. Ever think of becoming advocates with your competitors? Share wait lists and refer each other when you are full.

156. Work with a local coffee shop and see if they will name a coffee after your center one month.

157. Partner with local movie theaters to offer childcare to movie goers (like IKEA).

158. Offer huge incentives to your leadership for enrollment.

159. Baby's and dogs - need we say more? Pair them in pictures and post related content on social media to engage families.

160. Have a glow stick party for school agers!

GENERAL MARKETING

161. Host a day of kindness. Crest T-shirt's, hashtags, flyers, social media and more.

162. Host a luau and include Hawaiian shirts and photo booths.

163. If you have licensing visits that have ZERO violations - do a blog about it; share that news with families and prospective families.

164. Have a command station (electronic display) in the lobby that runs continuously showing amazing things about your center.

165. Evaluate the artwork on the walls in your hallways and in your classrooms; is there too much clutter? Is artwork outdated? Your walls make an impression on visitors and current families.

166. Have everyone dress for summer end of January to advertise summer camp.

167. Ask yourself, how can Child Care Biz Help - make enrolling new families easier?

168. Read P.R.O.F.I.T.S. Child Care Success Formula on how to master seven components for max profits at your child care center - chapter six is all on marketing: https://bit.ly/2XEWxty.

169. Coach your teachers on P.R.O.F.I.T.S. Child Care Success Formula Teacher Workbook so they know how they impact profits: https://bit.ly/2I3PtkF.

170. Sign up for the "Creative Retreat" with Child Care Biz Help and learn practical and creative marketing strategies to attract enrollment and recruitment.

171. Partner with the infant departments at hospital and clinics.

172. Partner with a lactation specialist.

173. Do you have a parking spot parents love to park because it is closest to the door? put a sign for 'family of the week/month' and put a drawing for a family to win the parking spot.

QUICK TIP

Increase marketing effectiveness by ensuring brand style and messaging is consistent on all advertising pieces.

174. Speak with certainty and confidence when trying to convert a tour into an enrollment - don't doubt what you have to offer!

175. Part of your marketing strategy should be to ensure you are priced appropriately. Evaluate your tuition prices every year. Are you competitive with your pricing?

176. Do you limit when potential families can tour, or do you have an open-door policy to let people tour anytime? When you limit your tour times you may give the perception.

177. Look at the outside of your building- are you missing areas to put logos or signage in view of the drive by?

178. Take something great you are doing, repackage it as something new and better.

179. If there is something that bothers you about industry, launch an awareness campaign to change it.

180. Define how you can be flexible in the childcare schedules you offer.

181. Make one day a week a specific tour day and really play it up every week!

182. Get branded mints made for families and employees to hand out.

183. Put a booth up at Farm n Fleet. Have a wheel of prizes for people to spin.

184. Offer to provide free childcare services at events.

185. Ice sculpture anyone? What would yours look like? Maybe you can get businesses near you to do the same to bring lots of traffic.

186. Partner with mortgage lenders. Give them treats at the bank and enrollment care packages for new family home buyers.

GENERAL MARKETING

187. Provide articles and resources on mindfulness to both your staff and families.

188. Partner with financial investors that work on family portfolio's in your community. What can you offer their clients? Have them come speak to your families.

189. Consider how you are partnering with your church or other churches in the community. They are often hosting family events you can participate in.

190. Does your window signage outside say what ages you service and what differentiates you?

191. Have random pop up tents outside - make sure to include bold signage advertising what is under the tent to draw people over.

192. Partner with home inspectors in your neighborhood.

193. Have a morning where the red carpet welcomes families. Go all out and take pictures of families dropping their kids off! Post live on social media.

194. Make the best first impression possible with prospects.

195. Sell Christmas ornaments that are branded for your center.

196. What about a hayride in your parking lot during the fall? Decorate the whole parking lot like a pumpkin patch.

197. Partner with a kid clothing store and have a sidewalk sale at your center on a beautiful day.

198. Have a book signing or famous child book author reading at your center.

199. Set up a "selfie wall" with a backdrop people can take pictures in front of. Change it out from time to time and put your store hashtag on it. Give customers discounts for posting to social media and tagging your store.

GENERAL MARKETING

200. Host Scholastic Book Fairs open to not only your families but anyone - create a Facebook event to share.

201. Have your families sell candy bars at their work and to their friends on behalf of the center to raise money for a good "child" cause.

202. Have a basket drawing of fun summer stuff for anyone that refers someone to summer camp.

203. Have your own version of "Happy Hour" - make it everything that makes you happy (smile face buttons, balloons, candy, karaoke).

204. Give out holiday survival kits.

205. Give exceptional customer service!

206. Sell your center if you lost passion for it!

207. Give your new families back packs or bags they can use when out and about.

208. How are you using your local park? Be active there!

209. Teach families how not to get sick during flu season.

210. Do blogs on super foods and how to incorporate super foods in children meals.

211. How are you networking as an owner to stay relevant in business? - don't let your knowledge go stale.

212. Find a group of child care professionals that are willing to be in a strategy type group with you.

213. Are you speaking to more than just the traditional family when you market?

214. As the owner, personally call the top 20% of your families to check in on them.

GENERAL MARKETING

215. If you have a trampoline park near you - consider ways you can cross market with them.

216. Video quick DIY crafts parents can do with their kids.

217. Organize "project connect" as a way to connect families with their children.

218. Every Friday do a quick video on family fun events for the weekend - tag those events so you get the added exposure.

219. Do you know someone that sells Thirty-one bags? Partner with them to cross market.

220. Get umbrellas made that have your logo on them.

221. Market school days off and brand these days and ask the local schools to help you promote.

222. Take advantage of seasons; It is always popular to give discounts during certain times of the year.

223. Transform your business card into a different shape, connect it to the fun of child care.

224. Include something special in the mundane - When you record an outgoing answering machine message, put in a memorable tip or message. Always change it. You can do the same thing for something as straightforward as your email signature.

225. We all love free stuff. People who really love great deals often go to deal sites as well as forums. There is usually a contest or sweepstake forum in there where you can include your contest.

226. Turn a negative into a positive- When something unfortunate happens as related to your brand and product and/or service, turn it into a positive.

GENERAL MARKETING

227. If there is no competition you can apply for or compete in, host your own competition to create buzz. Other companies would certainly want to win your award.

228. Create case studies- It is not as boring as it sounds. When you have satisfied customers, ask them to share their experience. The collection of these stories would bring credibility to your business and will allow you to get more customers.

229. Make a fun quiz- this is probably one of the easiest ways for you to establish some viral content and a good way to contact and connect with potential and current customer.

230. All industries have their secrets that people on the outside do not know. When is the best time to tour? How to build that strong teacher/parent relationship? How to negotiate fees?Do not be afraid to share your secrets.

231. Create free tools that families will find valuable and that will expand your brand.

232. Put together content that speaks to families from other sources. Get the parts you think would make up a great advice guide, for example. But remember, you must mention your sources.

233. How about working with your accountant to help bring you in new families?

234. Have your directors design their own pitch as to why a family should enroll; have each director present their pitch in a leadership meeting; How can they improve? What was great about it?

235. Do a S.W.O.T. analysis and share the results with your team - understand your company strengths, your opportunities, your threats, and weaknesses; how does each role play into the SWOT?

236. Tell your child care story. Write a blog, send out in a newsletter, do a press release.

237. Pay attention to your environmental practices and share your commitment to a clean environment as part of your philosophy.

GENERAL MARKETING

238. Give a tour that families can't say no too!

239. Make sure your teachers are also trained on the importance of their role in a tour.

240. Consider a phone script to help with income phone calls. Smile with your voice.

241. Create habits in your leadership team so they are consistent with following up on leads.

242. Learn to delegate so you have more time to devout toward enrollment follow-up.

243. Know why families leave your child care center and learn ways to grow from it and prevent it from happening.

244. Learn how to market to millennial parents: know where to find them, what matters to them, and don't forget Dad.

245. Teach your team on how to prospect new enrollments.

246. Conduct regular coaching on sales to your team becoming more productive, more confident and more skilled at prospecting and sales.

247. Improve how you communicate your expectations to your team so they know what is expected from them in terms of helping market the child care center.

248. Teach strategies on how to prioritize your day.

249. Hire leadership that is outgoing and not shy.

250. Place banners strategically around town that advertise your business.

251. Broadcast your enrollment goals visually so the team has a constant reminder.

252. Have contests between leadership to encourage positive competition to meet goals.

253. Model the behavior you want your team to demonstrate.

254. Do role play exercises to help your team get better at closing an enrollment.

255. Forecast enrollment so you know exactly how many spots you have available.

256. Have a mobile dog groomer offer grooming services once a month.

257. Train your staff to keep selling even if you have waiting lists; We must always portray a need for urgency!

258. Consider a guarantee you can give customers on your level of service and create a stamp for it to put everywhere.

259. Get a huge cookie made with your logo and feed it to your families; share the activities on social media and tag the company that made your cookie!

260. Are you clear who your target audience is for enrollment?

261. Embrace new ideas, behaviors and technologies.

262. It's not about customer loyalty any longer, it's about company loyalty to customers. How are you showing loyalty to your "Sweet Spot" customers?

263. Consider new technology partners to help you provide better options for your teachers, families and to market to new ones.

264. Make your brand of lotion and give as gifts to your employees and families - it's really easy to make! Put a custom label on it and give extras to families can share with their friends.

265. Revise your flyers often to keep things fresh and new.

QUICK TIP

Revise your website, especially your career page, often to keep things fresh and new.

GENERAL MARKETING

266. Have a bus you provide transportation in? Wrap it with a fun design/campaign that is eye catching and prompt people to call.

267. **Develop a loyalty program for parents. The longer they are enrolled, the more vacation days they get.**

268. Partner with local pizza places to put enrollment/recruitment fliers on their pizza boxes for a specific time frame.

269. Partner with local restaurants and supply coloring pages and crayons (with logo and enrollment/recruitment info) to give to families when they dine in.

270. Design mailers that speak to a specific campaign you are running; generally, need three months' worth of mailers to make an impact.

271. Use your center windows as advertising by designing eye catching window clings.

272. Sponsor a little league and have a banner to advertise your center.

273. Consider working with your local bank and design "bank bucks" to be handed out at the drive through.

274. Design a bookmark and have the library give out.

275. Always be "Tour Ready" and train your staff to be tour ready!

276. Utilize your vestibule/entrance to put branding materials.

277. Use your floor! Put decals or vinyl on your floor to engage teachers, families or students, take video and post on social.

GENERAL MARKETING

278. Write a guide to everything kid friendly that is local, see if you can get the Chamber on board to help with cost.

279. Do you have an area parent's magazine/newspaper? Be sure to place a couple of print ads each year, just to stay relevant. Take advantage of their online opportunities.

280. Do you have professionally designed and printed brochures? If not, now might be the time to get them and elevate your look.

281. When is the last time you issued a press release about a promotion, new location or event?

282. Find out the professions your families work in! Have them come talk to classrooms (3's, 4's, Pre-K, Camp) and give a fun presentation - post on website/social media.

283. Create a center calendar and get it printed, showcase students or classrooms on each month with the photo. sell. proceeds can go to buy more books (or other necessary supplies) at your center.

284. Does your community Chamber publish a business directory that you can be a part of?

285. Get a giant Instagram frame printed and use it as a prop for an event. make sure to create a good hashtag.

286. Tired of boring business cards? We talked about fun shapes earlier, how about considering using exciting texture or paper [look up the tiny cheese grater].

287. Get center bumper stickers and put them around town.

288. Make a tour packet to give to your tours.

289. Design branded folders for tour packets.

290. Put ad in high school programs and event guides.

GENERAL MARKETING

291. Place ad in your neighborhood magazine.

292. Have a roll of stickers printed and donate to doctor or dentist office to give away to kids. Make sure to get your logo on it.

293. Advertise in a church bulletin!

294. Work with a local coffee shop and see if they will use your branded coffee sleeves advertising an enrollment special.

295. Paint crazy designs that are large and bright in your center parking lot to attract attention.

296. Gym dressing rooms are great for flyers.

297. Put flyers in door hanger bags and put on homes.

298. Advertise through your voicemail message - put your latest special you're running in your voicemail.

299. Design posters that you change up occasionally to advertise things like your PreK program, Summer Camp, Enrollment Specials etc.

300. Put together a cool booklet on children's' milestone's and give them to your bank to hand out.

301. Make an annual alumni magazine that includes success stories of current and past students/families.

QUICK TIP

Hang up flyers at local stores your target market would likely visit. Many libraries have community bulletin boards, and display a posters on an easel in a lobby.

302. Create a parent network group - have "lead" parents reach out to new families to help them navigate starting at your location.

303. Get decals made for car windows that employees and parents can display that say they are proud to work at xxxx or proud to send my child to xxxx.

304. Give away gas cards at the local gas station and talk to people about your center - have a good bag to give which includes a flyer.

305. Get on the news! What can you do or say that is news worthy?

306. Hang up flyers at local stores your target market would visit.

307. Start and maintain a referral program to enroll new families.

308. Host a booth at park and recreation events; have games that appeal to kids you are targeting.

309. Take your business card everywhere and share it with potential families.

310. Ask your city if you can paint a mural with the children on a vacant wall.

310. Get sponsors on your camp shirts to not only raise additional money but also to gain additional exposure from the sponsors.

311. Volunteer as a company in local events or local needs and market what you are doing to help get exposure to enroll new families.

312. Find a park where you can plant a tree as a center and donate it. Consider a custom plaque on or near the donation.

313. Work with a local coupon company to be included in a new family welcome basket.

314. Make a list of local places your families visit so you can target those places to enroll.

GRASS ROOTS

316. Host a teacher car wash on a Saturday and wash cars in the neighborhood - provide free materials about your center.

317. Host a ribbon cutting with your local Chamber of Commerce to rededicate your center.

318. Don't under estimate the power of a hand-written letter...send a personalized thank you or thinking of you in the event of a family emergency.

319. Mail a congratulations card to families who welcome new babies, new pets or new home.

320. Bring back the penny wars! Have a competition between age groups or schools to see who can raise the most, pick a charity or local organization and donate it.

321. Anytime you donate money to someone, make sure to include a giant check for photo!

322. Don't forget about the importance of following up with prospective families. No time? Use Child Care Biz Help's SMAP to automate it.

323. Have you toured your competition lately to see what they are doing? We recommend doing this at least once a year.

324. Celebrate your birthday (day you opened) with a party to include cake, ice cream and the happy birthday song.

325. Give families free kites and host a kit flying event - have everyone wear t-shirts that have your center name on them.

326. Let the phone ring only ONCE. you don't want to miss those opportunities to engage a new family or teacher right away and ALWAYS answer with a smile.

327. Video your kids talking about why they love coming to your center; also use those statements and create a "child testimony" wall in your entrance and down your hallways.

328. Update your outdoor signage.

329. Design some sandwich board signage and put out to attract new enrollment.

330. Rent a cupcake truck - who doesn't want cupcakes?

331. Train your staff on how to "Pitch" what differentiates you.

332. Organize a neighborhood safety team in charge of keeping the neighborhood safe. Have employees attend events that are organized.

333. Hire "Another You" to take care of all your policies, procedures, handbooks and marketing needs; contact Child Care Biz Help.

334. Internally learn to celebrate wins as you hit milestones! This helps keep the momentum going!

335. Host a charity auction and donate the proceeds to a good cause.

336. Host a book resale event on a Saturday.

337. Put up a little free library at your entrance and encourage parents and the community to use it.

338. Play host to a toy swap where families can bring in gently used toys and swap with other families.

339. Create a coupon book with other business owners and give them away.

340. Host a clothing swap where families can bring in gently used clothing and swap with other families.

341. Get vinyl banners printed and get permission to put them up in high traffic areas, not just on your lot.

342. Organize "pop up playgrounds" and bring all the games and fun and interact with families on the weekend at the park.

343. Decorate public sidewalks with info/pictures about your center.

344. Hold a business card drawing for a prize (tuition credit, vacation coupons etc.).

345. New owner or new to the area with a new location? Go introduce yourself to other businesses and take them a goody bag.

346. Create a coloring book and give to local doctors and dentists with crayons for their waiting rooms.

347. Get some inexpensive tote bags with your logo on them and donate them to the library, be sure to include a flyer and coloring pages with your info on them.

348. Get corporate scholarships from local business partners for summer camp expenses and to offer camp scholarships; put the sponsors on your camp t-shirts.

349. Plant beautiful flowers near your entrance.

350. Start a woman's or men's coffee networking group and discuss different ways you can support each other's businesses; build in referral networking.

351. Brand your floor mats so you have a professional image for all new people that enter your building.

352. Give to get; think of things you can give to get something in return.

353. Help sponsor a lady's night with other businesses in your area - call it "a splash of positive" and pamper the attendees; great way to market your center.

354. Rent a dunk tank for a day and have fun getting dunked. Let your employees dunk you, let your families dunk your teachers; use to raise money for a charity or new program materials

355. Host an after-five networking event for others that want to network; have it at your facility and then inspire others to rotate and have it at their business.

356. Have a lemonade stand in the middle of the day! Have the kids make everything and run the stand - paint the stand and the signage too!

357. Fill up your bus with a million balloons and drive around town giving them out. Trust me, I rode in a bus with a lot of balloons and I never laughed so hard in my life. Try it!

358. Give your local Chamber of Commerce a pile of your brochures to hand out to new businesses.

359. Host a self-defense class or sponsor one at your local gym; gear the class toward not only women but children.

360. Rent a booth at your local farmers market; consider selling art work your children make; invite families to participate in the booth with you.

361. Provide free snacks to gymnast or dance groups during their tournaments and wear swag that shows off your center name.

362. When you go grocery shopping or school supply shopping, wear your company t-shirt or other attire.

363. Partner with a local "welcome wagon" group and have your brochures and information sent to new families that move into the area.

364. Find a teacher in another state that teachers' children the same age and be pen pals. don't forget to use technology to video chat and send letters back and forth. post on social.

365. Give a end of school year gift for Pre-K families. Consider seed packets with a label "we loved helping you grow".

366. Sit in a coffee shop all day with a friend and just wait to jump in on other people's conversations and get them to enroll!

367. Visit a pop-up beer garden and network for families.

368. Put your logo on balloons and use them everywhere.

369. Organize a baseball team with your teachers and sponsor the team. Pay for the entrance fee and the uniforms. Make sure the logo is on the shirts and caps.

370. Organize a volleyball team with your teachers, sponsor the team, and pay for the entrance fee and uniform shirts.

371. Have a block party with a couple other businesses on your block. Advertise it for at least a month to get the community excited about it.

372. Share flyers with a karate place to give to their families. Offer a special.

373. Host a car wash off premise. Give enrollment specials to people.

374. Face paint anywhere there are kids.

375. Take treats to nurses at hospitals. Leave business cards.

376. Host a "pay it forward" campaign and find ways to show appreciation to other business owners.

377. Drive your school bus to shop so people see your center name.

378. Host a yoga in the park once a month for anyone that wishes to attend; if you have a great outdoor and/or indoor space - have it at your center; this is a great way to gain exposure for enrollment.

379. Design Macarons in the shape of apples to represent being an educator; give as gifts to potential families during tours.

380. Rent a booth at the movie theater especially during kid movie showings.

QUICK TIP

Face paint anywhere there are kids. Use art students to paint gorgeous designs with high quality paints (glitter!) so the experience is special and memorable.

381. Allow a pop-up flower tent sell flowers in your parking lot.

382. Sell Christmas trees in your parking lot.

383. Partner with a local sub shop and give coupons for free registration to customers.

384. Do you have a restaurant near you that is not a chain restaurant? Partner together with them on everything!

385. Have Starbucks come hand out shots of espresso in the morning during coffee week.

386. Partner with local bakery to handout donuts and other pastries for National Donut Day!

387. Partner with local real estate agent(s) to give your brochures to families touring homes in the area.

388. Put new enrollment coupons in mass mailer that gets sent to every household in the community.

389. Put fliers on car windshields in local grocery store parking lots or business parking lots in your area.

ONLINE MARKETING

390. If any families or teachers have a rare condition or are passionate about a rare disease/ condition celebrate it each year to bring awareness - post on social media/write blog.

391. Analyze your website? Is it time to redo it?

392. Be creative with online photo contests and give a gift basket for the winner.

393. Pay Per Click Google ads.

394. Create Facebook Ads that have well written call to action focused content; send to a landing page that is well designed and collects information from the lead.

395. Boost Facebook posts after they have received high engagement for a few days.

396. Make sure you have online listings completed and ensure they are consistent (Yahoo, Bing, Yelp, Care.com, Great Schools, etc.).

397. Make sure you have a business LinkedIn Page.

398. Record a video highlighting different areas of your program and your USPs. put on website and social.

399. Write a new blog each week and share across all platforms.

400. Have an upcoming exciting announcement? Tease it on social for a few days (or weeks if you have them) to get people guessing.

401. Create an ebook to put on your website that people can download (great lead generation tool).

402. Ask a doctor, or other expert to guest blog; They can share it on their social and so can you!

403. Infographs are your friend! Create them full of great data and engaging pictures. When the content is good, they will get shared by your viewers.

404. Create instructional videos parents could use at home (preparing kid friendly meals, tying shoes, potty training, etc.).

405. Partner with a local business and share their content and ask them to do the same of yours. Be clear about expectations and what you will/won't share.

406. Have an expert rank your main keywords using onsite and offsite SEO.

407. Write a story for local publications to show yourself as an industry expert.

408. Have a photo booth day where families and stop and take goofy pics. Make sure the background has your company name; share on social media and have families share.

409. Have parents submit a child's "first" picture (first ice cream, first roller coaster ride, first snowman); compile and hold a contest on Facebook for the most likes. Parents will share.

410. Have a website that clearly defines what makes you unique.

411. Reviews, Reviews, Reviews.

412. Tell your story online about how you work hard to raise up new early education leaders and influence children's lives.

413. Have teachers write blogs about their classrooms or "spotlight" something special they did in their room that month.

414. Participate in throwback Thursday and post pictures from previous years (the older the better) be sure to use the hashtag #tbt.

415. Offer back to school enrollment special.

416. Latest video trend gone viral (lip syncs, dances, etc.) - record your own and challenge families or other centers to do it with you!

ONLINE MARKETING

417. Have a caption contest! Do you have a funny picture of a teacher or project gone wrong? Run a caption contest and pick a winner (get permission from teacher before doing it).

418. Make sure your URL structure is always optimized for search engines.

419. Consider custom landing pages for each campaign and use SMAP to track them. Contact Child Care Biz Help and find out how.

420. Use your current families email addresses to create look alike audiences on Facebook, so your ads target the right people.

421. Instagram! Use hashtags that are relevant to your business in your area (ask a teacher for help) remember 5-11 hashtags on each post are the goal.

422. Where do you rank on Google? It is good to know, and important to be towards the top. If you don't know, get familiar.

423. Know the best time to post on Facebook by looking at your insights. post during high traffic time so more people are likely to see it.

424. Create a hashtag like #ontheridehomefrom (CENTERNAME) and have families post a picture/story about what their child said they did that day on the way home.

425. Create a hashtag #roadtrip and have families post pictures of any trips they go on during the year - give families a flag/towel with your logo on to hold in pictures.

426. Go Facebook Live during events or if a teacher is doing a fun experiment in their classroom (be mindful of which children can be on social media and which ones can't).

427. Start a podcast on critical topics in child care-consider special guests (doctor, SLP, personal trainer etc.).

428. Utilize a chatbot on your Facebook page/website to auto respond.

429. Create a custom email signature for your families to add to their emails (i.e., My child attends the best child care center ever!).

430. Think of checklists you can make that families would find useful. Post and have them share.

431. Create an online parenting magazine. Doesn't have to be extensive, just useful facts, resources and maybe just consider publishing it quarterly or bi-annually.

432. Use quizzes to attract clicks and shares on social media.

433. Post a "Fun Fact Friday" on your website and Facebook page.

434. Never write a social media post without including a photo. There are a lot of free online tools you can use to make one.

435. Make sure your emails/website has social sharing options enabled.

436. Post articles on your company LinkedIn Page.

437. Create a badge to put on your website to celebrate how many years you have been in business if you are celebrating a milestone.

438. Do a Google 360-shoot to share on social media for a full online tour of your facility.

439. Use Canva to help make social media images, flyers, brochures, eBooks and more.

440. Host a Lego building challenge to your families to see who can build the tallest and craziest Lego creation; families should post on social media so other families can judge the winner.

441. The owner MUST do videos of why they own child care centers and why families should enroll.

442. Give major gifts to your staff when they get 5-star reviews - share those reviews everywhere!

ONLINE MARKETING

443. Have a drip campaign (automated email marketing) to keep in contact with prospective teachers or families and use SMAP to do it. Contact childcarebizhelp.com.

444. Recreate a fan favorite picture of children at your center...using teachers and caption it 'who did it better'.

445. Create an Instagram grid (individual pics that when put together make a much larger picture. these are fun and impactful.

446. Have photos of the owner and other leadership with their families doing things they love to do; this will show they are real people and allow for families and employees to connect with them on different level.

447. Share posts and blogs with parenting advice; be honest about your own personal experiences as a parent.

448. Share real stories about your business including milestones you hit, struggles you went through, along with your successes.

449. Share posts from other vendors that would impact your families and employees.

450. Really do something outrageous like raise a ton of money for a big cause and write a press release to get on the news.

451. Partner with a local smoothie shop or coffee shop and give free drinks away one more or afternoon; tag each other on social media doing it.

452. Research what kind of free publicity you can get? There are so many online options now!

453. Respond on other people's blogs as a child care industry expert and include your center name and/or web address.

454. Concentrate on authoritative backlinks from websites that have high credibility.

455. Create short helpful videos for new parents (how baby should sleep, how to keep a schedule, etc.).

456. Manage your online reputation, so you can make sure to respond to any positive or negative comments about your center.

457. Pay attention to your website analytics and make sure the pages people are visiting look the best.

458. Place online ads on Pandora.

459. Purchase pop up ads on popular apps.

460. Make sure your email signature and your staff's email signatures are branded, include a call to action, even link to testimonials.

461. Design a website landing page that specifically talks about the benefits your programs have for children.

462. Post on your materials and website what parents should expect to move up to the next age group. This is great SEO content plus it's a good way to prepare new families.

463. Review the area "above the fold" of your website - the area you first see when on your website homepage; does that space have your contact information, your unique selling proposition, and a call to action to get you to do something?

464. Put on a staff talent show for families, take footage of the event - use for enrollment.

465. Expand your LinkedIn networking with other professionals in your same community.

466. Use technology!

467. Do a video of the kids selling your center.

468. Have your business partners/vendors guest blog on topics families and/or teachers would be interested in.

469. Do blogs on bullying and how your team works with children and parents in this area.

470. Write a blog on biting and what your team does to prevent this.

471. Write a lead generating eBook on parenting nightmares and how a child care center partner can help.

472. Do you have any broken links on your website? If so, it's hurting your seo.

473. Do you know what keywords you should rank in?

474. Start advertising summer camp in January. Be full by February.

475. Write blogs pairing a student with a teacher and the bond they share.

476. Redo the verbiage on your tour page to really entice the viewer to act!

477. Is your website responsive?

478. When is the last time you viewed and understood your website analytics.

479. Make cake pops and offer a pop-up enrollment special! Do videos of things popping up.

480. Use Launch Now Agency to help you get on page one of search engines.

481. Sell positivity! What can you shout out about on social media that is positive?

482. Use clay to create a video story board of what it's like to work for your company - share on social media.

483. Ensure the content within your website has links to relevant external websites. Build relationships with companies that offer complementary services to your own such as schools and local kids sports teams, and then ask to trade links.

484. Start a YouTube channel and designate a playlist just for culture and why work at your center. Share it!

485. Video a fire drill to show how your team is prepared for disasters.

486. Have a photographer to professional photos for your website.

487. Change up your home page randomly to keep it relevant and current.

488. Pay for banner ads on websites that speak to mom's and/or mom's groups.

489. Have an M&M giveaway for the day; promote the day on Instagram and tag M&M.

490. Link internally to other relevant pages within your site to help with your onsite seo.

491. Do you know what is special about today specifically? Get on the bandwagon and talk about it and how you are incorporating in your center's day.

492. What does your about us page on your website say? Does it look and sound like everyone else's?

493. How are you using parent reviews on your website? Are they just boring testimonies that never change? What can you do that is unique?

494. Do you have a chat option on your website?

495. Make sure you have a summer camp landing page that clearly shows how much fun kids have, how to sign up and what a typical day looks like. Make sure to include urgency to sign-up by February 1st to get a spot.

496. Create a summer camp Facebook event on your Facebook so parents can share it; boost your summer camp Facebook event.

497. Don't forget the Google ad for summer camp along with organic SEO.

498. Blog about your summer camp and use keywords directed on summer camp searches.

499. Are you listed with the Better Business Bureau?

500. Become a member of the American Camp Association to publish your camp.

501. Write for a mom's group blog.

502. If you host an online contest, give participants more points of the share it!

503. Interview experts in the child care industry using a set questions. Share their answers through a blog post and how they related to the care you provide.

504. Make a funny 404 page- 404 pages are known as web pages that tell site visitors that the page they are searching for could not be found. Turn your 404 page to something funny so it could turn viral and be shared by friends.

505. If you attended an event like a conference or seminar for your industry, write about the information you gathered, what you thought was interesting, and the like. Other people might find them interesting as well. You can even use a hashtag for your efforts.

506. Create a Top Ten List! These are fun blogs and get good engagement. Maybe top 10 reason for group child care versus home care.

507. Share promotions of your team with the business journal.

508. Use Pinterest boards to enroll.

509. Send your monthly newsletter not just to current families but to prospective families in your pipeline.

510. Make sure your social media posts follow suggested guidelines: https://buffer.com/library/ideal-image-sizes-social-media-posts.

511. Use Eventbrite to advertise your free events.

512. Post events on Facebook events instead of just sharing an image on Facebook; then have families share the event.

513. Work with SoTellUs video reviews; it's a really easy way to collect reviews from families and teachers. Visit site here: https://sotellus.com/.

514. Advertise with your local recreation group so you can sponsor family type events they put on.

OFF THE WALL

515. Hold a contest for the most family referrals for the year and give away a family trip to Disney or some other family destination.

516. Design, purchase and give away center swag for families (bags, totes, water bottles).

517. Design and giveaway temporary logo tattoos!

518. Purchase spots on a radio and run a campaign (multiple months for best results).

519. Put up a billboard on a highway near your center.

520. Holding a fun event? Create a Snapchat Geo filter and encourage your guests to use it and share the images on social.

521. Write a book that will help families (i.e., importance of raising a child age 0-3).

522. Get a rubber chicken and pose it in funny places and countdown to summer camp.

523. Write a song about your center and record it, be sure to include a music video.

524. Take video testimonies of your families and put on your website, share on social media, have on a kiosk to display during a tour.

525. Develop the most off the wall perks and benefits package for your employees and advertise what you are doing (Think outside of the box).

526. Have your staff make a music video centered around your culture.

527. Adopt a highway.

528. Write your own children's book.

529. Rent a petting zoo for the day (don't forget to get a special event insurance certificate).

530. Hire clowns that walk around your parking lot all day and have a registration booth outside for people to come tour your center.

531. Come up with unique and eye-catching displays to put outside your building near the road - switch them up randomly and place enrollment and recruitment signs near it.

532. Create a center cook book of kid's recipes that are submitted by families.

533. Hire an amazing balloon guy and have him give out fun balloons in the parking lot as families leave for the day; tape the event and go live on social media.

534. Have some good singers? have them record all the kid's favorite songs and make a cd.

535. Anytime you have a special event, get special t-shirts made for everyone with your logo and something to go along with the event.

536. Have pens (good ones) made with logo and contact info with a special "code" on them. Have teachers/staff leave them at local businesses to get people in the door to win their "prize".

537. Put an enrollment ad/video in the previews at the local movie theatre.

538. Local movie theatres sometimes do business spotlights, take advantage and have your center spotlighted. have a representative there on weekends to talk to families.

539. Know all your family's birthdays (parents included) and give them a birthday card on their day (or mail it!).

540. Buy time on your local morning show to talk about something exciting happening at your center (new location, exciting program, unique opportunity).

541. Bring in massage therapists for a "spa" day for your teachers after hours or on a weekend.

542. Create a mascot for your center - make a costume and have someone dress up in costume at every event!

QUICK TIP

Consider in-house "field-trips". For example, have firefighters or police stop by with a firetruck or police car to show the kids.

543. Opening a new location? Offer a free year of tuition! be mindful of verbiage used.

544. Purchase and electronic message center to put near the road and display messages.

545. Invite a football celebrity to do an autograph signing at your center.

546. Auction of a teacher for a day to help at home on the weekends...they can help with a party, babysitting etc., and the center pays.

547. Organize flash mobs in the mall, at restaurants, parking lots.

548. Create animal ambassador's; Who can resist a cute puppy or kitten? Partner with a local rehoming shelter and encourage adoption alongside promoting your event!

549. World record attempt; Investigate world record attempts that relate to childcare. If there is a current record make a serious attempt to smash it in the lead up to the official event.

550. Send a personalized video to every family congratulating them, wishing them happy birthday, or happy holidays, etc., whatever the celebration may be.

551. Host your own stand-up comedy once a month virtually.

552. Partner with local news stations to be their child care expert. if anything, newsworthy happens about child care, they can reach out to you for comment.

553. Celebrate National Pi Day by giving away mini pies.

554. Create a Groupon for your center that new families can use.

555. Start a comic strip and publish everywhere; who knows, you might have the newest most popular comic!

556. Get custom made scratch off tickets made with your center name on them; have your staff hand them out to potential families.

557. Have a smores over the campfire night for families to attend and bring a guest.

558. Host a blood drive; Generally, a blood drive van can park in front of you center for a few hours during the day.

559. Make a list of your vendors and build in a referral program with them if they personally visit your center (like your FedEx or UPS driver).

560. Participate in a golf outing and network!

561. Use Fiverr for so many ways to create videos, do commercial clips, fun drawings, etc.

562. Make branded key chains for your employees and families.

563. Have playground balls printed with logo and website to give out at events and to prospective families.

564. Create an original theme song for your center.

565. Host a kid's chef night where kids challenge each other to prepare a meal for the teachers; do this in conjunction with a food/cooking enrichment program.

566. Be crazy different than everybody else!

OFF THE WALL

567. Evaluate where you could place your logo around your facility, your playground, your vehicles; Be smart and look for areas to sell your brand.

568. Host a children's fashion show.

569. Use puppets in a fun way. I'm sure you can find many goofy ways to incorporate them into your marketing.

570. Host a food art exhibit event; all participants must bring food shaped in goofy art.

571. Just learn how to ask for the enrollment.

572. Caffeine helps you do anything! Incorporate it!

573. Design beach towels as swag to give away to new families.

574. Offer fresh baked cookies to every tour that comes in the door. personalized cookies work too.

575. During super bowl time make your own outrageous commercial and share on social with a catchy heading like "the ad they didn't want you to see ".

576. Write a company jingle. The catchier the better.

577. Create a campaign intentionally breaking all the marketing rules that are current...go old school!

578. Do a complete playground redo with your staff and have a big reveal party on social media to celebrate.

579. Commission a plane to do a fly over banner.

580. Partner with a local maternity store to put your info out.

581. Personalized popsicles with your name/logo on the stick, hand out at event.

582. Invite a popular sports mascot to your center for photo ops.

583. Host a Veteran's Day program that is open to the public to attend.

584. Rent out your local pool or aquatic center for the day for your families only to attend (depending on size of center, families may be able to bring a guest family).

585. Rent out an entire theater for a special showing of a popular movie. Create photo opportunities to put outside the theatre so parents can share on social.

586. Support your local Girl Scouts by allowing them to put up a cookie booth outside your center.

587. Get Yeti's for everyone on your team...make sure they are branded.

588. Pay for ads on YouTube.

589. Live in a city with public transportation? Pay to wrap a bus.

590. Re imagine your playground-turn your jungle gym into a castle, boat, rocketship or bus.

591. If your city does concerts in the park, get your children a night to perform songs, skits.

592. Host a poker/casino night at your center, proceeds benefit a local charity.

593. Create a center animated cartoon using Toonly about crazy things that happen during the day.

594. Offer Gift certificates that can be given as a gift to expectant mothers, etc.

595. Get a meal named after your center at a local diner.

596. Purchase branded napkin ring holders and donate to a local diner.

597. **Rent a cotton candy machine and hand it out.**

598. Get a Kona ice truck to visit your center.

599. Have a big giveaway event for summer like a couple bicycles - advertise it everywhere and have the giveaway at the end of the day on a Friday.

600. What about custom license plate holders! Give them away to all your families to put on their cars.

601. Get ties for dads that have your centers logo and tag line on it.

602. Make a custom screen saver and provide to your families to use on their work computers.

603. Send out mass texts to your families offering pop up referral specials.

604. Host a snack party and have families invite a friend; offer an enrollment special for the referred friend and a tuition credit to the family that brought the friend.

605. What does your vestibule entrance look like? Are you making a welcoming impression? How about an inspirational quote posted every day?

606. Ever think of parachuting? Raise money for kids of you do it! Take sponsors, hype it up.

607. Just smile and talk to people.

608. Stay off your phone in line at places and just talk with people near you.

609. Analyze your parking lot; is the asphalt faded, does it need to be resurfaced? Sometime your parking lot can look old and cracked and that will give a poor impression about your center.

610. Rent a wind machine and put various tuition coupons in it. Have a day we're everyone gets one shot in there. Really play it up!

611. Consider opening a second or overnight shift.

612. Love what you do, and it will rub off on others. They will be attracted to where you are!

613. Learn to laugh at the small things!

614. Food! Need I say more? It solves everything.

615. Go to Tony Robbins conference and build your confidence.

616. Lean on good friends to help you through stressful times.

617. Auction off a month of cleaning service for the next 10 enrollments.

618. Have a dance party. If anything, it will change your mindset.

619. Host a lady's spa night with all your teachers and families. Have people sign up and reserve the whole spa is you need. Doesn't mean you pay for everyone.

620. Ask yourself, how can Child Care Biz Help make my center perform at its peak?

621. Take a walk in the park and clear your head.

622. Read Justina's Unplugged Guide on how to recharge yourself: https://bit.ly/2K50apo.

623. Have I mentioned iced coffee! It's amazing and it helps make the brain work fast!

624. Design temporary artwork to sit outside your building to draw attention to your space.

625. Make a documentary about the life of a center director.

626. Workout your stress! Clear your mind and attack your recruitment problems when you are refreshed.

627. Try out for America's Got Talent.

OFF THE WALL

628. When is the last time you met with your banker to talk about how to take your business to the next level!

629. Sign up for "Help a Reporter Out" (HARO).

630. Hold contest for a specific cause and "winners" get to throw a pie in the Director or Teachers faces.

631. Instead of taking your children to work day, host a bring your parent to school day at your location to show your parents all the hard work your teachers do and all the fun the children have. (have different days for different age groups).

632. What if you purchased a book mobile and drove around town; promote reading and sell your center.

633. Get your street named after your center.

634. Can you put together a fun zone at the mall that you can sponsor.

635. Find a seamstress to offer free alternations every quarter for families.

636. Offer random live music in the parking lot during the summer at the end of the day.

637. Do you have bushes outside on your property? Can you shape them into funny shapes?

638. If your center is not open yet, offer a drawing for a huge prize to anyone that enrolls with your center before day 1. Consider grandfathering tuition for all founding students.

639. Offer a month of free tuition after someone has been enrolled for a year.

640. Host a breakfast potluck and invite families to take breakfast on the go.

641. Love what you do and encourage those around you to do the same!

OFF THE WALL

642. Paint your concrete. So fun colors outside your entrance.

643. Paint a mural with families.

644. Hold a competition - any kind will do!

645. Donate spa certificates to random enrollments.

646. Host an after hours fitness class for parents and their children.

647. Use your bathroom to talk about your culture and to give a positive vibe.

648. Have a local musician write a jingle for your center.

649. Get your summer camp on the radio because of the community cause initiative that is included in your camp mission.

650. Think about creating your very own comics online to show funny or weird parts of your business.

651. Give away a cruise to the family that help enroll the newest families during the course of a year.

652. Create Bitmoji' s of everyone and have fun with them in your marketing materials, on your website, social media.

653. Start a morning minute podcast to get parents started off the right way as they drop their kids off in the morning; Maybe it's an inspirational podcast?

654. Create a product like a "Bark Box" that families can order themselves or other families (a monthly subscription); the box can include games for children, family activities, etc.

655. Owners - don't forget about your Directors. They are always worried about the day to day activities of the center and are always looking out for others instead of themselves - don't let them burnout.

656. Hand out Sachets & Mini Air Fresheners with your own scent - http://www.scentisphere.com.

657. Be thankful!

658. Don't let fear hold you back; we often doubt ourselves, fear the worse outcome, and even fear the inabilities of our team. Squash fear - it has no place in your work and personal life.

659. **Be BOLD! Know your center is amazing.**

660. Hire a coach to help your team see themselves as sales Rockstar's.

661. Have a servant heart - Caring about the success of your team more than personal gain.

662. Maybe it's time to buy a competitor!

663. Stay on top of new businesses that come into your community by asking your local village administrator who got new permits and approvals.

664. Use Grub Hub to deliver food to businesses you want to cross market with.

665. Connect with other local businesses and collaborate on prize packages for a huge collaborative contest to collect leads.

666. Understand the digital needs of you families and teachers and provide them.

667. Repackage child care both from the family perspective and the employee.

668. In addition to enrollment metrics, track retention, satisfaction, and health of culture.

669. Love what you do and be contagious to everyone you meet! Now go be awesome and impact your community, your families, your employees!

670. Make your own "Best Place to Work" award - create a logo and post everywhere including on print, shirts, marketing materials.

PROGRAMS

671. Each month highlight a career/profession and have a parent come talk to classrooms about what they do.

672. Create amazing enrichment programs that you can brand and advertise to help gain enrollment.

673. Spotlight your nutrition program through videos, blogs, special events.

674. Spotlight your curriculum through videos, blogs, special events.

675. Create parent referral network to use for prospective families.

676. Find new ways to be innovative so you can differentiate yourself; maybe you have new educational technology families would be drawn too?

677. Invest in your staff's professional development and require continuous learning so you have the most passionate teachers.

678. Start a meal program where parents can pre-purchase meals twice a week to take home when they pick up their child(ren); sell this benefit in all your marketing.

679. Start a community garden where families can help maintain and food can be given back to the community and to your families.

680. Use Hopping-In to generate additional revenue.

681. Have you instituted a proven process to create raving fans.

682. Conduct exit interviews for families when they leave to determine what you can do better!

PROGRAMS

683. Celebrate staff birthdays/anniversaries with small gifts (under $10), post on Facebook or other platform and signage in their classroom.

684. Create a family of the month program. encourage families to apply to win, pick a winner and they get a goody basket.

685. Take care of any outside maintenance issues around your facility.

686. Have an essay contest that older children can participate in and have a winner and award ceremony.

687. Offer a couple scholarships for enrollment.

688. Offer a couple scholarships toward college credits for staff; increase scholarship levels based on longevity of employment.

689. Know your employees' talents and use them to make your programs the best.

690. Know your family's talents and use them to make your programs the best.

691. Take a look at your nutrition program; how can you highlight healthy meals, your chef, or other aspects of your program?

692. Host trainings for your staff that they normally wouldn't want to pay for (like how to be debt free, how to live without fear).

693. Spend money on a curriculum coach for your staff to help them have the best programs in their classrooms possible.

694. Read leadership books and encourage your team to do the same whether they are in a leadership role or not.

695. Host a kid bop karaoke Saturday.

696. Blog about each one of your core values over the course of several months and give examples on how your employees live those values.

697. Organize a father daughter dance!

698. Organize a talent show for the kids.

699. Build on your teams' strengths so you can have the best programs ever. This will create a natural continuous enrollment stream.

700. Have your employees sing a song asking families to complete a survey (i.e., Let it go can be sung as Let us know) - then you can get top participation and learn the most on how to improve and be the best. Who knows, maybe your video will go viral?

701. Brand your summer camp to keep children coming back each year. Change the theme every year to keep people interested.

702. If you have someone that designs jewelry, have them design a unique piece of jewelry just for your brand. Sell it and use the proceeds to make improvements in your programs.

703. Offer a mid-morning toddler play class for mom's looking for an afternoon break in the day.

704. Do you have an eye doctor that specializes in children's eye care; consider sharing materials with them and asking them to teach a workshop for your families.

705. Consider an event that shows off cultural diversity and invite the community to share in the performance.

QUICK TIP

Schedule parent-teacher meetings to check in with parents - find out how they feel about teachers, programing, and if they have any concerns about their child's development.

706. Evaluate how you are using your billboards in the hallways. Do they look professional or do they look like the kids put them together?

707. Have a local karate place teach an enrichment program for your kids.

708. Offer a new and unique type of enrichment program.

709. Hype how you help kids with their homework!

710. Have an etiquette enrichment class!

711. Encourage your families to smile every day when they drop off and pick up their children.

712. Build friendships with families and staff.

713. Is your kitchen clean? Tours and families should feel the kitchen is a good representation of your cleanliness standards.

714. Is your bathroom clean? Tours and families should feel the bathroom is a good representation to your cleanliness standards.

715. Work with your local farm on how to incorporate some local foods into your center menu - even your snack menu.

716. Have military veterans speak at your center to teach on community and patriotism.

717. Interview your camp instructors and let them share what camp will be like.

718. Interview your PreK teacher on why they are so passionate about teaching and what they intend to accomplish during the PreK school year.

719. Can you expand your camp to a separate pre-teen camp focused on activities for the pre-teen age only.

720. STEAM is now expected in summer camp - is your program on board?

721. Empower your staff to be advocates for your center, to own their classrooms and to live up to their full potential.

722. Use technology to limit paperwork so you have more time to spend with your staff, bettering your programs and enjoying your work.

723. Give detailed and constructive feedback to your team when they aren't hitting goals or if they aren't running programs like you expect.

724. Brainstorm new revenue generating activities you can have at your center. Maybe you teach school agers skills such as gardening, carpentry, cooking, car repairs, money, job interviewing, coping with failure.

725. Teach kids how to play and be creative again!

726. What are you doing to remain relevant in today's market? Businesses must constantly adapt their products, services, and marketing strategy to compete and remain relevant to the consumer.

727. Review your global influence and how you are bringing that influence into the classroom.

728. Be professional but not boring! What can you do that is unusual in the child care industry that speaks to your target market or even just the kids?

RECRUITMENT/RETENTION

729. Never stop hiring!

730. Go ALL OUT for Teacher Appreciation week. Plan something special each day of the week and have parents get involved. Post on social media for potential recruits.

731. Develop a loyalty program for teachers, the longer they are employed the better the rewards.

732. Design colorful and informative banner flags and put outside property advertising recruitment - go bold and colorful!

733. Partner with nearby Colleges & Universities with Education programs.

734. Create benefits flyers and go and speak at local colleges to answer questions about jobs you offer.

735. Make goofy hiring banner flags and say you are interested in crazy energetic teachers.

736. Host practicum students at your center-hire on after graduation.

737. Dress up as a hot dog and hold a "we're hiring sign".

738. Record a video of your leadership team telling why you should work for your company; put on career page and social media.

739. Host a career fair at night.

740. Speak at your local schools to gain recruitment.

741. Start a substitute teacher business to help recruit and earn additional income.

742. Record a video of a typical day as a teacher - but do it from "behind the scenes" and make it funny and all about your culture.

743. Volunteer as a company in local events or local needs and market what you are doing to help recruit.

744. Share success stories of growth your staff has made due to professional development and continuous learning.

745. Implement Dream Manager program to inspire your team to dream and work at obtaining life goals.

746. Create ambassadors (past employees that have left on good terms) - pay them $100 to hand out flyers at local places teachers may visit.

747. Try Google pay-per-click ads to get new employees. Write a really funny ad that appears when someone is searching for a teaching job.

748. Go back through your list of good employees that left on good terms and ask them to come back.

749. Make sure you have a solid on-boarding and retention program, so you spend less time recruiting.

750. Make a list of local places your employees visit so you can target those places to recruit.

751. Blog about culture related topics that would inspire people to want to work for your company.

752. Take your business card everywhere and share it with potential teachers.

753. Show appreciation to your staff (not just about gifts) and capture that appreciation on video or in word and share.

754. Make sure you have a solid interview process in place that hires based on culture.

755. Host a "virtual" career fair and boost the event on Facebook, Instagram and LinkedIn; invite key members of your team and a few teachers to speak at the virtual event.

RECRUITMENT/RETENTION 

756. Host a flip cup tournament at work (with water of course) - post on social media with the hashtag #wehavefunatwork and #workhardplayhard.

757. Develop career paths for employees to continuously be growing with your company - market this on website, benefits package and recruitment.

758. Host a red-carpet event for employees.

759. Host needed trainings/continuing education for teachers at your center. Invite teachers from other centers to come.

760. Have teachers share recruitment Facebook posts to their personal pages to help widen your search.

761. Offer sign on bonus to qualified teachers, pay half at start & half at 90 days.

762. Give a $5 Starbucks card to prospective employees after they have an in-person interview as a thank you.

763. Do a 'Stats Board' for new employees on their first day (favorites, fun facts, etc.).

764. Plan an annual or bi-annual "retreat" for your teachers to bond, brainstorm and de-stress together as a team.

765. Video "Minute to Win It" competition during staff meetings to show how much fun you have together. Post on website and social media platforms.

766. Have the owner, HR director or other impactful speaker, speak at local child care conferences. this can be a great way to find new staff.

767. Put out yard signs that say you're hiring and put balloons around them to attract people's attention.

768. Treat every candidate like a customer! Great employers provide a transparent, efficient and organized interview process, communicating with applicants every step of the way (yes, even if they don't get the job!).

769. When coming up with benefits, don't just think insurance, think wellness; specifically, both mental and physical wellness.

770. Conduct exit interviews for employees when they leave to determine what you can do better!

771. Referral programs to recruit teachers.

772. Give new teachers a "swag bag" on their last day of orientation before they are in the classroom that has t-shirt, pens, teacher bag, notebook, etc.

773. Did a teacher have a baby, get married, graduate? Celebrate their wins with signage in the center and on social.

774. Have an internal mission statement? put in on the wall in your staff break room.

775. Work with a local college to host college level classes at night to help your teachers get certifications.

776. For staff that have been with you the longest, reward them with 2 round trip tickets to anywhere they want to go.

777. Host a P.R.O.F.I.T.S. training for your staff after you read the book, so they know the importance of your business too.

778. Have a teacher that has hit the salary cap? consider putting a bonus structure in place or give them added responsibility.

779. Have top performing teachers participate in Leadership series events hosted in your area.

780. Host a clothing swap for staff to exchange clothing.

RECRUITMENT/RETENTION 

781. Start a book club for staff...pick a variety of books.

782. Start a leadership book club where you read self-improvement books and talk about that.

783. Schedule time for the owner and/or director to take each staff member to lunch annually.

784. Buy staff lunch on their first day.

785. Work with a partner that can help you recruit teachers and other key personnel in your organization; visit childcarebizhelp.com.

786. Uplift your teaching staff so they know how important they are and how much they impact the lives of children.

787. Do a video on the "behind the scenes" of child care and how you are a great place to work.

788. Create an online teacher magazine.

789. Have a member of your leadership cook breakfast for the center once a month.

QUICK TIP

Attitude is everything. Skills can be taught, so when hiring, put personality fit first.

790. Create a company LinkedIn Page and write about your culture and show pictures of your work environment to peak interest of passive lookers.

791. Make sure your employee breakroom is awesome! When interviewing, take potential candidates to see it. A great breakroom is generally representative of culture climate.

792. Host an early education trivia night and invite teachers to attend to win a major prize.

793. Don't be afraid to hire the Starbucks drive through if they are fabulous!

794. Get custom made scratch off tickets made with your center name on them; have your staff hand them out to potential employees.

795. Get core value coins made and give to staff when they demonstrate living core values; share pictures of employee receiving these coins on social media and on the career page.

796. Create a FAQ's sheet of reasons why employees enjoy working at your center.

797. Host a paint night with your staff as a team building event -share experience to help with recruitment.

798. Use "Slack" to communicate with your teachers - uplift them, encourage them, and share ways to be their best.

799. Join and become active in your local child care association. Use the association to help train your team, learn best practices, and to recruit.

800. Participate in a career fair at your local university to recruit new talent; make sure your booth stands out from everyone else - think of ways you can draw people to your space.

801. Promote healthy living with staff by having a walking group after work or a workout buddy program. This can help accountability and build relationships by being healthy.

802. Create a YouTube channel where your location has its own "tv series". Highlight teachers, creative classrooms, and other activities that sets your center apart from competition.

803. Focus on non-monetary benefits and communicate those visually and with words.

804. The owner MUST do videos of why they value their employees and why people should come work for them.

805. Advertise reverse interviews; place an ad for prospective employees to come interview with your kids' panel.

RECRUITMENT/RETENTION 

806. Have your staff write a book called - "Why My Work Rules" - use this eBook to attract new talent but also to build momentum with your current team.

807. Concentrate on your Top 20% of employees so they can be strong leaders for the rest of the group. Equip them, get them pushing the vision, and soon you won't need to hire more teachers because people will want to stay.

808. Host a training conference and invite teachers from all over to attend.

809. Have a vision board night with your staff so they can create personal and work-related vision boards.

810. Go on a food tour with your team and take a lot of fun pictures!

811. Use Basecamp to keep track of all your to do items.

812. Are your employees all in the right seat (The Energy Bus Book).

813. Design custom pop up sockets and give as gifts to your employees.

814. Host a mindfulness seminar for your staff.

815. Always incorporate a team building or other collaborative piece in each staff meeting - share the experience in a blog.

816. Praise should come from the top down. Praise your director and leadership and in turn they will praise the staff.

817. Give each classroom a budget and take a weekend trip to IKEA and let them shop. document with photos and don't forget to eat the Swedish meatballs.

818. Host a weekend retreat for your staff to unplug and enjoy the outdoors and team building time.

819. Go to an escape room with your staff. Break into groups and see who can get our the quickest.

820. Attend or host a murder mystery dinner. bonus points if you have to dress up.

821. Video teachers performing the correct way to complete specific policies and procedures in your facility (handwashing, diaper changes, etc.), have new staff watch as a training piece. Much less boring than reading.

822. Create fun awards to give to your staff during a staff meeting (pushing the boundaries of business causal, historian, late is the new on time, etc.).

823. No Call-In-Program. For each week a teacher does not call in the get a ticket, at the end of the predetermined time (1 year) they get to enter their tickets into a drawing for a variety of things (TVs, cash, trips, a boat, gift cards)...they must keep track of their own tickets and no reissues allowed (change ticket each year to prevent reusing).

824. Get larger Easter eggs and hide paper in them with different gifts to benefit teachers (lunch on the director, 30 mins classroom coverage, extra planning time, $5-dollar tree gift cards, etc.), hide in teacher only areas.

825. Host a cookie exchange for staff during the holidays.

826. Secret Santa/White Elephant/Brown Bag Game.

827. Apply to education grants or have your teachers apply.

828. Partner with the high school to provide placement/on the job training for their child development class.

829. Go all out for an amazing holiday celebration for your staff. Fancy dinner, Great entertainment, Thoughtful gifts etc.

830. Play a licensing, accreditation, center policy game of Jeopardy at a staff meeting.

RECRUITMENT/RETENTION 

831. Sit in a coffee shop all day with a friend and just wait to jump in on other people's conversations and get them to apply for a job!

832. Visit a pop-up beer garden and network for teachers.

833. Market to seniors, chances are your community will have a large portion of them who have experience in education or would love to be part of early education in their retirement years.

834. Work with your local high school and hire people that may have disabilities where they can maybe help in different areas of your center.

835. Pay attention to the mental wellness of the employees in your center; they will be better at their jobs and easier to retain.

836. Work with a local coffee shop and see if they will use your branded coffee sleeves advertising employment.

837. Partner with your Village Center if they have a lot of senior activities and see if you can speak to the group about working part time hours at your center.

838. Get in touch with school districts and the person who handles when teachers phase out and/or retire; see if you can get face time with the retirees before they finish their teaching contract.

839. Collaborating in group sports as a team to demonstrate a unified group. This is a great way to attract new employees.

840. Look at your recruitment ads and ask yourself if there is anything crazy you can say in your intro to attract prospects to read it? I.e., Work Among Winners! Our Team of Rockstar's is Waiting for You!

841. Publish articles in LinkedIn on mental wellness and explain some techniques you can do for teachers to ease work stress.

842. Put on a staff talent show for families, take footage of the event - use for recruitment.

843. On your career page, have a video from the Director saying who they are and why they love their employees.

844. Ask your teachers why they like coming to work: look at ways you can continue to meet those needs.

845. Host your own amazing race and advertise the whole thing. It's fun and can attract publicity and fun!

846. Organize a college and career group on campus. Up-n-coming teachers! Meet weekly on topics concerning students looking to become teachers.

847. Do group trainings with nearby centers to cut on costs of training.

848. Host babysitting classes.

849. Mentor preteens.

850. Spend money on great training for your staff.

851. Have state of the company meetings quarterly with staff to keep them informed of company goals and vision.

852. Give huge bonus to teachers for referring teachers.

853. Offer huge incentives to leadership for retention of employees!

854. See if you need to revise your interview questions.

855. Is it time to revise your job descriptions?

RECRUITMENT/RETENTION

856. Where do 60+ people hang out? Find out and recruit!

857. Participate in an iron man competition as a team.

858. Tell friends your hiring and ask them to help you recruit.

859. Take classes on health and wellness so you can meet those needs of employees.

860. Hire interns over the summer to get your center name in the community.

861. Pray for help recruiting teachers.

862. Is it time to reevaluate your review process? consider adding a mental wellness section.

863. Fill plastic light bulbs with yellow candy and tie a ribbon that says- "your future is bright with us"- use at career fair.

864. Have a slide show that represents your amazing culture run on an iPad or computer at a career fair.

865. Have a separate blog just for employees and prospects. This blog feed is on the career page.

866. Watch what you post on social media. Really play up happy employees - not just receiving gifts but truly looking happy!

867. Host a podcast on teacher hacks. Be the channel teachers want to listen too.

868. Offer a student loan payback program based on longevity.

869. Have you looked at who the director is and if they are the reason you are losing employees.

870. Design a career pathing program.

871. Payout company bonus when enrollment and retention numbers are hit and base payment on longevity.

872. You ever just take an employee out to lunch to say they are doing a great job?

873. Consider hiring an HR person to handle recruitment and on-boarding.

874. Don't just appreciate your staff during teacher appreciation week.

875. Evaluate what you're doing to acclimate a new hire to your center culture before someone even starts day one.

876. Don't forget Child Care Biz Help can help with a variety of tasks, such as recruiting!

877. Read child care surveys to ensure you are offering competitive benefits and salaries.

878. Host a yoga in the park once a month for anyone that wishes to attend; if you have a great outdoor and/or indoor space - have it at your center; this is a great way to gain exposure for recruitment.

879. Read Traction by Gino Wickman.

880. Read Dream Manager by Matthew Kelly.

881. Provide a hot chocolate bar & decorate cookies.

882. Bring branded party glasses for your employees to any party you organize.

883. Host a multicultural food festival & gift exchange.

RECRUITMENT/RETENTION 

884. Create outrageous ice cream sundaes; Decorate sundaes first, then judge and eat the best ice cream sundaes.

885. Decorate Bbusiness-related ornaments for your office Christmas tree.

886. Organize a SUMO throw down at your next staff meeting.

887. Cater in a healthy breakfast bar to start your employee's day off right!

888. Host a Slo-Mo Party to demonstrate your fun culture: https://bit.ly/2wGzrXg.

889. Celebrate Unicorn Day – April 9.

890. If you meet all your major company goals - rent this house for employees to join you at: vrbo.com/4109211ha.

891. Hatchet throwing is kind of the new thing, how about an employee outing to get some aggressions out.

892. Have a brainstorm wall and only let people write on it on Friday's.

893. Choose an employee (who has exemplified a company value) to draw a name out of a bowl and the pair gets to go to lunch on the company.

894. Hire a personal trainer or bootcamp instructor to host a bootcamp session at your center.

895. Teach an ab strengthening class after the center closes - 2x a week.

896. Have different team members lead informative presentations to teach something new or reinforce our culture. Some of the topics could be "How to be a brand ambassador" or "How to live out our company core values."

897. Send out a Google Survey asking people to choose from 3 movies, select the winner, and play it after work. Don't forget the popcorn!

898. Playing games with your staff during meetings or off time is a great way to lighten the mood and improve moral, lip sync battle anyone?

899. Organize a fitness challenge in your company to promote health and wellness.

900. Take your top performers out to breakfast. They will be your biggest cheerleaders!

901. Give gift cards to craft store to top performers.

902. Have recruits train in every classroom to see what room they prefer.

903. Create onboarding videos for areas that have want to make sure your expectations are upheld (talking with families, child transitions, safety/security, etc.).

904. Do you have a parking spot your teaching staff are constantly trying to get? Put a sign for 'Teacher of the month" and assign it to a different teacher every month to park there.

905. Have your current leadership team take the Gallup Strengths Analysis to see where their strengths are, and to identify where you may need work, this will help when looking for new hires.

906. Have all candidates for leadership positions take the Gallup Strength Assessment to make sure they are a good fit and see if they will fill in where your current team is lacking.

907. Send press releases to Early Childhood Publications when you have teachers that achieve major milestones to highlight their victory (finish credential, graduate college, etc.).

908. Write a list why someone 50+ years old would come work for your company. Add to recruiting materials.

909. Establish some benefits and perks that 50+ ages employees would value.

QUICK TIP

A good manager makes sure every person on the team has the support and tools needed to thrive in their role.

RECRUITMENT/RETENTION

910. Get a fun wheel that employees can soon for fun stuff at staff meetings like time off, money, jeans day.

911. Be willing to pay more for employees that are willing to work harder to fill time slots.

912. Make ad language say looking for all ages employees from high school to mature and retired.

913. To attract an age-diverse candidate pool, your website photos should include both young and old employees.

914. Maturity. Judgment. Work ethic. This is the value experienced workers can bring to your workforce. When younger and older employees work together, everyone is more productive.

915. Use AARPS job board and HireMaturity to hire 50+.

916. Instead of thinking of cultural fit as age-related, look for people who are motivated to work with your company, dedicated to lifelong learning, and show a history of being creative and adaptable.

917. Consider what impacts our employees at home to help them better cope with stress.

918. Walk the walk don't just talk it!

919. Be willing to train older candidates on skills and other requirements needed to be included in ratios.

920. Can't stress enough to look at how you treat employees during the first 30 days of their employment. Think about personal touches you can make as an owner and/or Director to get to them.

921. Since it's so hard to get people to show up for their interviews, how about texting them 3 intro question to screen them; then schedule a face to face.

922. Since it's so hard to get people to show up for their interviews, make a super funny video you can text back to candidates once you have an interview scheduled to get their curiosity going.

923. Define how you can be flexible in the employment schedules you offer.

924. Have pop up career events. Put a chair outside with balloons and interview banners. Make it fun and free food for anyone that interviews.

925. Take your employees to paint ball and take pics of all the fun.

926. How happy are the people at your company? Do you need to consider cleaning house to get rid of toxic people?

927. When you work on your SEO efforts, don't forget recruitment words to add to your list of important keywords: best place to work, great place to work, employment in xxx, teaching jobs in xxx.

928. Make the best first impression possibly with recruits.

929. Consider hiring with longevity in mind... offer a huge cash bonus if the candidate stays one year, then two years, etc.

930. Consider paying for a simple short commercial that is wacky about the kind of people that work for you.

931. What a billboard for hiring teachers? Make sure to depict the different ages and diversity of the people you hire - but make it fun!

932. Recruit using Spotify.

RECRUITMENT/RETENTION 

933. Develop a "most wanted" hiring campaign - make posters and social media images that give ransoms for finding the most wanted talent you are trying to hire.

934. Speak to the passive job seeker that may not know they want to switch jobs yet.

935. Do a song parody like "Adele's Hello" and have your team sing Hello to new teachers.

936. Create hiring memes.

937. Host a teacher Resource Book fair and open to not only your teachers but to any other teacher in the surrounding community - create Facebook event to share.

938. When is the last time you gave medals to staff for being amazing.

939. Make sure your team knows they are the best at what they do.

940. Offer an extra week of vacation when an employee has been with you over a year.

941. Pay for a random employee's monthly food budget just out of the blue.

942. What about a teacher feud competition during a staff meeting? Have fun with it and incorporate training topics in the questions.

943. Encourage your staff to just smile.

944. Do one on one interviews with your teachers. Highlight something about them or their teachings.

945. Dedicate a small budget toward staff pop up fun times.

946. Bonfire for staff at your house? S'mores and fellowship.

947. Simply give employee staff reviews on time and they won't leave you! They will remain happy and refer others!

948. Be an owner that cares about their employees.

949. What is the TOP 3 Reasons someone should work for you? Make t-shirts for your staff to wear.

950. Give your staff nice jackets with your center information on them to wear in public.

951. Teach your staff how to beat depression. Maybe bring in a speaker to teach on it at a staff meeting.

952. Create "I Use My Talents for..." t-shirts for staff that use their talents to help your center.

953. Ever consider having a social captain that helps facilitate getting employees outside of work hours.

954. As the owner, personally call the top 20% of your teachers to check in on them.

955. Give teachers in your local school district survival kits at the beginning of the school year.

956. Give your teachers survival kits at the beginning of the new school year.

957. Be the best boss you can be, so you attract the best employees there are!

958. Believe that you truly are the best place to work!

959. Have an option Saturday work day where employees can come in and be part of a brainstorming session on how to recruit teachers; No idea is turned down! Great way to unify as a team toward one cause.

960. College campuses are a great way to do pop up recruitment and giveaway tents. Really play it up big with games, food, and plenty of swag.

RECRUITMENT/RETENTION 

961. Give Craigslist another shot.

962. Pay attention to employees at other businesses; they don't have to already be teacher - hire based on personality and customer service.

963. Design a custom Snapchat geo filter with a local college in mind; Feature it with some fun graphics and your careers email address.

964. Use LinkedIn creatively: do teacher specific keyword searches on LinkedIn, followed by InMail's to highly targeted individuals.

965. Host networking events in venues your target recruit would attend: what about an open MIC night?

966. Create a Snaplication: A Snapchat user can view a 10-second video ad about how great it is to work at your company and if the job prospect wants to know more, have a link to your career page in Snapchat and to the job application.

967. Give paid apprenticeships to potential teachers that aren't old enough to be included in ratio's yet. Get them hooked on your center!

968. Raid the talent at your competitors.

969. The best way to reach recruiting targets is to use the communications approaches that they favor. And since over 70% of mobile phone users use text, it makes sense to conduct initial interviews using text messaging.

970. Use Skype for initial interviews to reduce the stress of face to face interviews and having to travel.

971. Seniorjobbank.org to hire professionals over 50!

972. Team up with AARP to hire seniors; People who are 55 and older will make up 24.8% of the workforce by 2026, projects the U.S. Bureau of Labor Statistics.

973. Make it easy for employees to share job openings on social media.

974. To find good employees, try talking to your best hires. Find out how they found you. See if they have any referrals - people they would enjoy working with.

975. Look for niche job boards that focus teachers.

976. Outsource your recruitment process.

977. Use Pinterest boards to recruit.

978. Learn to delegate so you have more time to devout toward recruiting efforts.

979. Create an initiative to invite a friend that could be a potential teacher to your next staff meeting; to anyone that brings someone, they get an extra 2 hours of personal time.

980. Teach your team on how to prospect new teachers.

981. Bring in a life coach to help your staff better cope with their personal lives.

982. Think about new experiences you can offer your teachers; what will make them feel more at peace, love work more, feel less stressed? People hardly forget a great customer experience and will happily tell other people about it.

983. Consider a guarantee you can give your employees on your dedication to making an exceptional workplace - create a stamp for it and place it everywhere.

984. Are you clear who your target audience is for recruitment?

985. Rewire your workforce with a customer-first mindset.

986. Don't hire out of desperation!

RECRUITMENT/RETENTION

987. Start a "I Walk Unified" campaign by looking up the distance to a variety of places and encourage your staff to walk the miles to get there. Log the miles as a team, and when you hit certain milestones (400 miles, 1,001 miles), celebrate. If the miles represent how far it would be to Nashville, attend a concert in the park. If you walk enough miles to Mexico, consider a taco and margarita night.

988. Host open interviews at an ice cream shop, give candidates a coupon for discounted ice cream after interview.

989. Have a local hockey team? Go to a game as a group.

990. Institute a bring to friend to work day for someone you think will make a good teacher, have them volunteer in the classroom (supply lunch, do necessary background checks).

991. Put a hiring ad in the previews at the local movie theatre.

992. Have employees vote each year on an additional benefit they get for one year, this will give them a voice, and owners a way to see what they want (extra day off, extended lunch, birthday off, lunch with the boss Etc).

993. Find out where families work and ask if you can post flyers at their companies for enrollment and recruiting purposes.

994. Always have a pipelines of potential leadership team members; mentoring future leaders is so important to reducing the need to recruit.

995. Become involved with local technical college early childhood education program. Be a mentor, teach classes even.

996. Become a train-the-trainer certified and teach classes at your center for continuing education hours not just for your team but any center in the area.

997. Mentor students at your local high schools interested in early childhood education.

998. Replenish now hiring posters monthly at community boards (coffee shops, library, grocery store, high schools, colleges).

999. Create a YouTube channel that goes behind the scenes of being a teacher at your center.

1000. Hold open interviews once a month where you accept walk ins and do interviews on the spots.

1001.

Believe you are the best employer out there. If you lead with this mindset, you are going to attract top talent. When you build a team around you that is equally passionate and energetic about the early education industry, there is no telling what you will be able to achieve as a child care center.

Know your bigger purpose!

Made in the USA
Columbia, SC
06 August 2019